JOEL C. ROSENBERG
INSIDE THE REVOLUTION
STUDY GUIDE

TYNDALE HOUSE PUBLISHERS, INC.,
CAROL STREAM, ILLINOIS

Visit Tyndale's exciting Web site at www.tyndale.com

TYNDALE and Tyndale's quill logo are registered trademarks of Tyndale House Publishers, Inc.

Inside the Revolution Study Guide: How the Followers of Jihad, Jefferson & Jesus Are Battling to Dominate the Middle East and Transform the World

Copyright © 2009 by Joel C. Rosenberg. All rights reserved.

Cover photo of Osama bin Laden copyright © by epa/Corbis. All rights reserved.

Cover illustration of Thomas Jefferson copyright © by Rembrandt Peale/Getty Images. All rights reserved.

Cover illustration of Jesus used by permission of Bridgeman Art Library. All rights reserved.

Author photo copyright © 2005 by Joel C. Rosenberg. All rights reserved.

Study questions developed by Jennifer Lamont Leo.

Designed by Dean H. Renninger.

Quoted excerpts are taken from *Inside the Revolution*, © 2009 by Joel C. Rosenberg. Used by permission.

Unless otherwise marked, scripture quotations are taken from the *New American Standard Bible*®, copyright © 1960, 1962, 1963, 1968, 1971, 1972, 1973, 1975, 1977, 1995 by The Lockman Foundation. Used by permission.

Some scripture quotations are taken from the HOLY BIBLE, NEW INTERNATIONAL VERSION®. NIV®. Copyright © 1973, 1978, 1984 by International Bible Society. Used by permission of Zondervan. All rights reserved.

ISBN 978-1-4143-3325-0

Printed in the United States of America

15 14 13 12 11 10 09
7   6   5   4   3   2   1

contents

Author's Note / v
Introduction: Not "If" but "When" / 1

PART ONE:
the RADICALS

CHAPTER 01: Worst-Case Scenario / 9
CHAPTER 02: "Islam Is the Answer; Jihad Is the Way" / 13
CHAPTER 03: The Theology of the Radicals / 19
CHAPTER 04: "We Were Asleep" / 23
CHAPTER 05: Tragedy at Desert One / 27
CHAPTER 06: "We Must Export Our Revolution" / 31
CHAPTER 07: Christmas in Kabul / 35
CHAPTER 08: Declaring War on America / 39
CHAPTER 09: Unleashing the Islamic Bomb / 43
CHAPTER 10: Terror High / 47
CHAPTER 11: Revolution 2.0 / 55
CHAPTER 12: Making Way for the Mahdi / 59
CHAPTER 13: The Road Ahead / 63

PART TWO:
the REFORMERS

CHAPTER 14: "Islam Is the Answer, but Jihad Is Not the Way" / 69
CHAPTER 15: The Theology of the Reformers / 73

CHAPTER 16: The Defector / 77
CHAPTER 17: Meet Hamid Karzai / 81
CHAPTER 18: Karzai's Mission / 85
CHAPTER 19: "We Are Fighting Islamic Fascists" / 89
CHAPTER 20: Meet Jalal Talabani / 93
CHAPTER 21: Talabani's Test / 97
CHAPTER 22: The King and I / 103
CHAPTER 23: The Moroccan Model / 107

PART THREE:
the REVIVALISTS

CHAPTER 24: "Islam Is Not the Answer, and Jihad Is Not the Way; Jesus Is the Way" / 113
CHAPTER 25: The Big, Untold Story—Part One / 119
CHAPTER 26: The Big, Untold Story—Part Two / 123
CHAPTER 27: The Air War / 127
CHAPTER 28: The Ground War—Part One / 131
CHAPTER 29: The Ground War—Part Two / 135
CHAPTER 30: The Theology of the Revivalists / 139
CHAPTER 31: Making Way for the Messiah / 145
CHAPTER 32: Join the Revolution / 151

Afterword / 161
Loving Muslims to Christ / 163
Recommended Reading / 173

author's note

WHEN YOU HEAR the word *Muslim*, what images come to your mind?

Angry young men shouting epithets about America and Israel? Silent women shrouded in heavy black fabric—and quite possibly strapped with explosives? Cold-hearted terrorists slamming jets into office buildings? Hypersensitive fanatics in an uproar over some Danish cartoons?

Or people beloved by God, created in His image and for whom He weeps?

The Bible says that God loves every man, woman, and child in the world, Jew and Gentile. The Bible makes it clear that God offers His free gift of salvation to everyone who will believe in Jesus Christ. What's more, as you will see in the pages ahead, the Bible commands us to love our neighbors and our enemies, regardless of their ethnic and religious background.

Yet, when we read about new Radical Muslim threats to our country, and learn of U.S. and allied forces being wounded and killed in Muslim countries, and see rockets and missiles from Muslim terrorist groups raining down on Israel, and hear Iranian Muslim leaders vowing to annihilate the United States and Israel, is it any wonder that many people around the world—including followers of Jesus Christ—can often become worried, frustrated, suspicious, even angry?

Now, more than ever, we must understand the enormous war of ideas under way in the Muslim world and the unprecedented soul-searching under way in Muslim hearts. Something is happening throughout Islamic society that has never happened before in all of human history, and so little of it is being reported by the mainstream media or being taken seriously by the Church. My prayer, therefore, is that *Inside the Revolution* and this companion study guide will help you develop a greater understanding of—and compassion for—this complex and multifaceted people and God's plan and purpose for their lives, and for yours.

WHY USE THIS STUDY GUIDE?
After years of crisscrossing throughout North Africa and the Middle East, I wrote this study guide for five reasons:

1. To help readers of *Inside the Revolution*—as well as my earlier nonfiction book, *Epicenter*—get the most out of these two books and develop a clearer and deeper understanding of the trend lines in the Islamic world at a moment when the clash between Islam, Judaism, and Christianity is reaching its most dangerous stage.
2. To create a resource that will stimulate small group studies and discussions about why the Islamic Revolution occurred in Iran in 1979, how Washington missed it, how the Revolution was exported throughout the Middle East and around the world, and why there are now three revolutions under way—those led by the Radicals, the Reformers, and the Revivalists—not just one.
3. To help readers examine events in the Muslim world not just through the lenses of geopolitics and economics but also through the "third lens" of Scripture.
4. To inspire true followers of Jesus Christ to develop a heart of compassion for Muslims at home and abroad, help them to see how many millions of Muslims are turning to faith in Jesus Christ, and challenge them to ask God what role they are supposed to play in the remarkable spiritual revolution and harvest of souls now under way.
5. To mobilize a global movement of millions of followers of Jesus Christ to pray daily, knowledgeably, and faithfully for the peace of Jerusalem, for the salvation of Muslims, and for the spread of the Church throughout the epicenter.

HOW TO GET THE MOST FROM YOUR STUDY OF *INSIDE THE REVOLUTION*

Before you begin the study, take stock of the situation in your own mind and heart. Spend some time thinking through your current thoughts and feelings about Muslims. Consider the images you've seen on television or in newspapers and magazines. Mull over things you may have heard your family, friends, and coworkers say about Muslims. Then ask God for eyes to see and ears to hear what He wants you to learn.

When you're ready to begin, I recommend that you set aside at least thirty minutes a day, five days a week, to read a chapter of *Inside the Revolution*, work on the questions in this guide, look up the relevant Scripture passages, and pray about what you've read. This daily discipline will help you get the most out of the material and help you establish the wise habit of a daily appointment with the living God, if you don't have such an appointment already.

You can certainly do this study on your own. But for maximum impact, I would recommend that you meet with a friend or small group once a week to compare notes, discuss the issues, and pray together. You may not always agree with the views and perspectives others have on this material, but you will more than likely think more deeply and more carefully if you don't study in isolation. Plus, you'll have more fun and hopefully develop stronger friendships along the way.

As you work through the study, some of the information you'll learn may be disturbing or unsettling to you. So bear in mind as you proceed that God loves you and has a wonderful plan for your life (John 3:16, John 10:10, and Jeremiah 29:11-14). God is in control of all things, and His will cannot be thwarted (Job 42:2). You can rejoice in everything and pray about everything, knowing that God stands ready to give you peace that passes all understanding (Philippians 4:4-7). Jesus will always be with you, no matter what, if you have truly given your life to Him (Matthew 28:18-20). And best of all, Jesus is coming back for you, perhaps sooner than you can possibly imagine (John 14:1-3).

Indeed, it is quite possible that He has led you to read *Inside the Revolution* and to complete this study "for such a time as this" (Esther 4:14).

May God bless you on your journey and draw you closer to His heart than ever before.

Joel C. Rosenberg
WASHINGTON, D.C.
MARCH 2009

INTRODUCTION
NOT "IF" BUT "WHEN"

"We are rapidly approaching the most dangerous moment in the history of the Iranian Revolution."
Inside the Revolution, page xi

1. Why are you doing this study of *Inside the Revolution*? What are you most hoping to get out of your study?

   _____

   _____

   _____

   _____

2. Why do you think it is important for Westerners in general, and Christians in particular, to learn about the political, military, economic, and spiritual forces within Islam?

   _____

   _____

   _____

   _____

3. Read Luke 12:54-56. Why does Jesus so strongly rebuke His followers for not analyzing "this present time"? How might this command of Jesus relate to staying informed about what's going on around the world, especially in the Middle East?

_____

_____

_____

_____

4. Write down three facts you know about Islam. Where did you learn these facts?

_____

_____

_____

_____

5. Now write down three questions about Islam that you have been curious about.

_____

_____

_____

6. On page xi, I suggest that Iran is approaching its most dangerous moment since 1979. Do you think that's true?

Why or why not? If it is true, what are the implications for those of us who live in the West?

_____

_____

_____

_____

7. On page xii, I suggest that "the leaders of Iran believe that Allah is on their side, the wind is at their back, and the end of Judeo-Christian civilization as we know it is near. I believe just the opposite." What do *you* believe, and why?

_____

_____

_____

8. On page xiv, I argue that "what [the Radicals] need most—what they pray for most of all—is Western ignorance, apathy, and lack of moral clarity." List some examples of this condition. What factors do you think have contributed to this problem in the United States and Europe? How can it be rectified?

_____

_____

_____

_____

9. What are the three groups of people in the Muslim world who are waging their own revolutions? List and briefly describe each of these groups.

10. What three groups of people in the epicenter are non-revolutionary in nature? List and briefly describe each of these groups.

11. From what you've learned so far, which group is the largest? Which group(s) pose the most serious threat to Judeo-Christian civilization?

12. Which hold out the greatest hope for a secure and peaceful future?

13. Were any of the groups surprising to you? If so, why?

14. Take some time now to pray for the leaders of our country as they seek to understand the dynamics in the modern Middle East and protect us and our allies.

the RADICALS

PART ONE

CHAPTER ONE
WORST-CASE SCENARIO

"The bottom line: time is running out."
Inside the Revolution, page 16

1. Discuss how the failure to rescue the American Embassy hostages in Tehran, the Russian retreat from Afghanistan, and the Black Hawk Down incident constituted "propaganda windfalls" for Radical Muslim terrorists.

_____

_____

_____

_____

2. What's going on in the minds of the Radicals? What are their motivations for robbing, killing, and destroying?

_____

_____

_____

3. The vast majority of the world's Muslims have no desire to wage jihad (holy war) against the West or Israel or to annihilate Judeo-Christian civilization. That said, how serious is the threat against the West from Radical Muslims? How seriously do Western governments appear to be taking that threat? Why?

_____

_____

_____

_____

4. What are General Boykin's top five worst-case scenarios?

_____

_____

_____

_____

5. Which scenario seems the most dangerous to you? Which appears to be the most imminent? Explain your responses.

_____

_____

_____

_____

6. Do you think that war is an effective means of deterring Radical terrorists? Do you think that diplomatic efforts would be more effective? Why or why not?

_____

_____

_____

7. How can you be praying for our military leaders and for our armed forces during this global war against Radical Islamic terrorism?

_____

_____

_____

8. Take some time now to pray for our military.

_____

_____

_____

9. As you read this section on the Radicals, you may find your spirit sapped from time to time. I know that as I pored over hate-filled speeches and reviewed dismal and tragic histories, I found myself getting discouraged. That is why it is so important to spend time each day in the Scriptures, getting to know the God of the Bible, who loves us and has a wonderful plan and purpose for our lives. Our hope as followers of Jesus

Christ comes from knowing God personally, knowing that He is in charge, knowing that His character and plans are both loving and trustworthy. Read Romans 5:1-8. What do you learn about God's love for you? What do you learn about the hope that He offers you?

_____

_____

_____

10. What is the connection between trials and hope? Spend some time thanking the Lord for the trials you are facing and the assurance that in Him we have unshakable hope.

_____

_____

_____

11. Read Hebrews 6:9-20. What does God promise in this passage? What is your part in taking hold of this promise?

_____

_____

_____

12. Spend some time now praying for those who are caught in the cross fire, living in places of oppression and darkness. Fight on your knees for those who need hope.

CHAPTER TWO
"ISLAM IS THE ANSWER; JIHAD IS THE WAY"

> *"We have decided and are determined to argue and prove that violence is at the heart of Islam."*
>
> Muhammad Taghi Mesbah Yazdi, high-ranking Muslim cleric and spiritual advisor to Mahmoud Ahmadinejad (*Inside the Revolution*, page 36)

1. Do you agree that "there are far too many in positions of American national leadership and in the media who either are not studying the Radicals carefully or simply are not taking them seriously" (p. 21)? Why or why not?

   _____

   _____

   _____

2. Did the statements of then senator Barack Obama about Iran (pp. 21–22) concern you? How do you think President Obama is approaching Iran now?

   _____

   _____

   _____

3. Based on your reading of *Inside the Revolution,* what are some of the most important points you hope the leaders of our government will come to understand?

4. Do you agree with Ted Koppel and Ted Turner that Iran should be allowed to have nuclear weapons? Why or why not?

5. Had you ever read these quotes of Radical Islamic leaders before (p. 23–28)? Do you feel the mainstream media is doing enough to report such quotes? Why or why not?

6. Why is the soul-searching going on throughout the Muslim world so important? Why do so many Muslims have a

"deep-seated feeling of shame, humiliation, failure" and so forth (p. 28)?

_____

_____

_____

_____

7. Discuss the roots of the Radicals' murderous anger and intention to destroy the Judeo-Christian world. How did the following historical events contribute to their current ideology?

    European trade-route circumvention of the Islamic world

    _____

    _____

    The dissolution of the Ottoman Empire

    _____

    _____

    _____

    The founding of the modern State of Israel in 1948

    _____

    _____

The Six-Day War of 1967

_____

_____

The Yom Kippur War of 1973

_____

_____

8. What does the Radicals' mantra—"Islam is the answer, and jihad is the way"—really mean? What are the Radicals' ultimate objectives?

_____

_____

_____

9. In this chapter, we have seen the power of the Radicals to incite violence through their sermons and speeches. Read Proverbs 30:13-14. What kind of man is the Bible describing? How does such a man "devour the afflicted from the earth" through his language?

_____

_____

_____

10. Read James 3 and consider the language of the Radicals. What are the word pictures for the tongue in these verses?

   _____

   _____

   _____

   _____

11. Describe the contrast between godly wisdom and worldly wisdom and what it produces.

   _____

   _____

   _____

   _____

12. Take some time to read and pray through Psalm 31 as you seek the Lord for protection from evil people and evil tongues.

CHAPTER THREE
THE THEOLOGY OF THE RADICALS

"While it is certainly accurate to say that the vast majority of Muslims are peaceful people, is it also true that Islam itself is an intrinsically peaceful religion?"
Inside the Revolution, page 41

1. Do you agree with my assessment that the vast majority of Muslims are not violent?

   _____

   _____

   _____

2. Do you believe Islam itself, based on the teaching of the Qur'an and the *hadiths*, is a religion of peace or a religion of violence? Why are there such different interpretations of the same writings?

   _____

   _____

   _____

3. According to various Muslim scholars, what is the difference between Greater Jihad and Lesser Jihad? Which form of jihad do the Radicals adhere to?

4. What do the Radicals believe that performing acts of violence in the name of Allah will do for them?

5. What do I mean on page 48, where I write, "Islam is a works-based religion"? What is the "51 percent solution"?

6. Can Muslims find assurance of salvation? Why or why not?

7. What is the Radicals' view of martyrdom?

8. What are some of the differences you see between what Muhammad did and taught and what Jesus did and taught?

9. Violence is a virtue as portrayed in the Qur'anic verses cited in this chapter. Read the passages below and describe the biblical view of violence, as well as Jesus' teachings about how to live lives of peace.

   - *Proverbs 1:8-19*
   - *Proverbs 16:29*
   - *Isaiah 53:7-9*

- *Matthew 5:5*
- *Matthew 5:9*
- *Titus 3:1-2*

_____

_____

_____

_____

10. In the Isaiah passage, how is the coming Messiah described? How did Jesus fulfill such prophecies?

_____

_____

_____

_____

11. In Matthew 5:9, what did Jesus mean when He said, "Blessed are the peacemakers"? How are the followers of Jesus supposed to emulate the model that he set for them?

_____

_____

_____

_____

CHAPTER FOUR
"WE WERE ASLEEP"

"Iran is an island of stability in one of the more troubled areas of the world."
Former U. S. president Jimmy Carter (*Inside the Revolution*, page 54)

1. If you are old enough to remember the late 1970s, what do you remember about the situation in Iran in those days?

   _____

   _____

   _____

   _____

2. How did the United States move from being a trusted ally of Iran in the 1950s to a hated enemy by 1979?

   _____

   _____

   _____

   _____

3. How was it possible that President Carter and the Central Intelligence Agency could so badly have missed what was happening in Iran?

4. How was the ayatollah signaling and preparing for the coming Revolution?

5. What risks are there today that Washington is again misreading the situation in Iran? What are the potential costs of miscalculating this time?

6. Some leaders in Washington admitted to being "asleep" to the Islamic Revolution in 1979. Read Matthew 24:42–25:13. What does Jesus tell His followers to do so they will not miss important and world-changing events?

_____

_____

_____

_____

7. Read 1 Corinthians 16:13-14 and Ephesians 6:18. How does the apostle Paul instruct followers of Jesus to live amid danger and threat?

_____

_____

_____

_____

8. Read 1 Peter 5:8-10. What are the apostle Peter's instructions to us?

_____

_____

_____

_____

9. What are practical steps that you and your family can take to be ready, be alert, be prepared?

10. Sometimes it feels like the wicked will always prosper and succeed, and this can be unnerving, especially in the age of Radical Islam. Take some time to read through Psalm 37. List the promises God makes us in this chapter. What does David mean when he refers to the "man of peace" in verse 37?

11. List what a righteous man is to do in the face of evil.

12. Pray through this psalm, thank the Lord that we do not need to fret when evil seems to prosper, and ask the Lord for the courage to be a man or woman of peace.

CHAPTER FIVE
TRAGEDY AT DESERT ONE

"'We're going to have to scrub the mission.'"
Delta Force commander Col. Charlie Beckwith (*Inside the Revolution*, page 78)

1. Discuss what happened during Delta Force's failed attempt to rescue the hostages in Iran.

   _____

   _____

   _____

   _____

2. What factors contributed to the failure? Which factors were unavoidable? Which could have been avoided?

   _____

   _____

   _____

   _____

3. What do you think the U.S. military learned from the Desert One fiasco?

4. What effect did the failure of Operation Eagle Claw have on U.S.–Iran relations?

5. It is so hard to face this type of tragic failure, especially when the mission is so noble and important. It can be hard to understand why God allows things like this to happen. Read the story of Joseph in Genesis 37, 39–50. What happens to Joseph?

6. What was Joseph's perspective on all his trials?

7. What does Joseph tell us in Genesis 50:19-24 about God's perfect plan in the face of evil?

8. What does God tell the Jewish people in Jeremiah 29:11-14 about his love and plan for their lives in the face of evil?

9. Read Job 42:1-2. What do we learn about God and His plans?

10. Take some time to pray for the oppressed people of Iran. Pray that they would discover God's love and perfect plan for their lives through His Son, the Lord Jesus Christ.

11. Pray for those on dangerous missions for the cause of righteousness right now. Pray Psalm 91 for them.

12. Thank the Lord for the trials in your life and take some time to meditate on how the Lord has turned past trials into blessings.

CHAPTER SIX
"WE MUST EXPORT OUR REVOLUTION"

"The Americans were now in retreat, all because of one driver willing to give up his life to kill others. This was a model, [the jihadists] concluded, that had to be replicated."
Inside the Revolution, page 88

1. Describe what happened at the bombing of the U.S. Marines barracks in Beirut in 1983.

   _____

   _____

   _____

   _____

2. What new terrorist tactic was introduced to the American public during this bombing?

   _____

   _____

   _____

3. Who took credit for the bombing? Why? What was Iran's involvement?

4. How would you handle the loss of a loved one after a suicide bombing or other terrorist attack? Could you ever forgive?

5. Why does God sometimes allow innocent people to suffer?

6. Who is Sheikh Hassan Nasrallah, and what does he want?

7. How is Nasrallah's view of the End Times shaping Hezbollah's foreign policy? Why is this dangerous?

_____

_____

_____

8. The story of the Beirut bombing is so disheartening and painful. How can we possibly forgive those who commit such crimes? Read these passages and write down what you learn about justice and forgiveness.

   - *Micah 6:8*
   - *Luke 6:27-37*
   - *Luke 11:1-4*
   - *Romans 12:14-21*

_____

_____

_____

_____

9. Spend some time praying for those who have been deeply wronged in the Middle East. Pray that they will find comfort and peace in trusting that God's justice is perfect.

CHAPTER SEVEN
CHRISTMAS IN KABUL

"1979 was not a good year for the CIA."
Inside the Revolution, page 97

1. How did the CIA miss the Soviet invasion of Afghanistan?

   _____

   _____

   _____

   _____

2. What does this tell us about Washington's ability to correctly assess the present and accurately anticipate the near future?

   _____

   _____

   _____

   _____

   _____

3. While reading this chapter, did you learn anything about Osama bin Laden or al Qaeda that you didn't already know? Any surprises?

4. What were the early influences in Osama bin Laden's life that may have contributed to his actions in adulthood?

5. Why was the U.S.S.R so interested in controlling Afghanistan?

6. What does *al Qaeda* mean? What does this group stand for? What factors have made it grow and flourish?

7. On what date was al Qaeda created? Why is this significant?

8. Did you realize bin Laden was so young when he created al Qaeda? What does that say about a single young person's ability to change the world for good or evil if he or she is passionate about a certain set of beliefs?

9. On page 109, I note that bin Laden has sought to effectively form "'Jihad, Inc.,' a multinational corporation dedicated to destroying Judeo-Christian civilization and imposing Sharia law on the entire planet." What do you think the United States and Europe would be like under Sharia law?

10. Read Jeremiah 1:4-10. What does the Bible say about the power of young people to join the God of Abraham, Isaac, and Jacob in changing the world?

_____

_____

_____

11. The apostle Paul understood the power of training young people to become game-changers. What were his instructions to Timothy, his young protégé, in 2 Timothy 2:1-4?

_____

_____

_____

12. What did Paul mean by being a "good soldier of Christ Jesus"? In light of previous Scriptures that we have looked at, could Paul have meant Christ followers should be violent or aggressive? Why or why not?

_____

_____

_____

13. Are you available to be used by God to shape the lives of young men and women for good rather than evil? Read Psalm 1. Pray for the young men and women in your life, in your church, in your country, in the countries of the Middle East—that they may follow Psalm 1's prescription for the right path to take.

CHAPTER EIGHT
DECLARING WAR ON AMERICA

"'We . . . call on every Muslim who believes in God and wishes to be rewarded to comply with God's order to kill the Americans.'"
Osama bin Laden (*Inside the Revolution*, page 118)

1. How many "disciples" did Osama bin Laden have around him when he created al Qaeda? What was their plan? Why did it grow so quickly?

   _____

   _____

   _____

   _____

2. How did the Soviet withdrawal from Afghanistan contribute to the growth of al Qaeda?

   _____

   _____

   _____

3. What was the disagreement between Abdullah Azzam and Ayman al-Zawahiri over strategy? With whom did bin Laden side? What happened to Azzam?

4. Why did al Qaeda get involved in jihadist operations against the United States in Somalia? How was the withdrawal of American forces from Somalia interpreted by bin Laden?

5. How old was bin Laden when he issued his "Declaration of War against the United States" (pp. 116–117)? What was his immediate objective?

6. What was his long-term objective?

7. How many jihadists did al Qaeda train upon moving their base of operations from Sudan to Afghanistan? Why was this significant?

8. As we learn about the development and growth of al Qaeda, we should ask ourselves if we as Christians are having a deep and intentional impact for God on this world. How were Paul and his companions described in Acts 17, and specifically verse six?

9. As followers of Jesus Christ, what is the mission that we have been given? Write out Matthew 28:18-20.

_____

_____

_____

10. Of all the things Jesus instructs His disciples to do in this passage, why does He specifically tell them to make disciples of *all* nations? Does this include dangerous, difficult, and deadly nations? Where do we get the power to accomplish such a mission?

_____

_____

_____

11. In the partnership (for evil) among Azzam, bin Laden, and al-Zawahiri, we saw "livid" disagreements, "deeply offended" people, and eventually murder as they jockeyed for positions. Read Psalm 133:1 and Ephesians 4:1-6. How are followers of Christ supposed to live and operate together in contrast to the Radicals?

_____

_____

_____

12. Spend some time praying for Christian leaders in your church and around the world to work together with humility and unity. Pray for believers to have a determined and passionate focus on evangelism and discipleship.

CHAPTER NINE
UNLEASHING THE ISLAMIC BOMB

"'I was responsible for the 9/11 Operation, from A to Z.'"
Khalid Sheikh Mohammed (*Inside the Revolution*, page 127)

1. Who was Khalid Sheikh Mohammed (KSM)? What was his connection to bin Laden?

2. Do you agree with me that KSM was "sheer evil" (p. 121)? Why or why not?

3. Do you believe that evil is a real force in history? How would you define evil? How would you recognize it if you saw it?

_____

_____

_____

4. Did you learn anything from this chapter about the events of September 11, 2001, that you didn't already know?

_____

_____

_____

5. What were your thoughts as you were reading KSM's list of "accomplishments" (pp. 126–129)?

_____

_____

_____

6. What is the ultimate objective of bin Laden and al Qaeda?

_____

_____

_____

7. What are they hoping to obtain, and what do they want to do with it when they get it?

8. How serious is this threat, in your view?

9. Is Washington sufficiently focused on this threat? Are the American people?

10. What does the Bible say about evil in Psalm 140?

11. Read Proverbs 1:10-19. What is the fate of those who practice evil?

_____

_____

_____

12. As we learn about bin Laden and KSM, it is morally appalling to note their lack of concern for human life. They dream of the deaths of millions of innocent people. What do the following verses tell you about God's value on life?

    - *Exodus 20:13*
    - *Exodus 23:7*
    - *Jeremiah 7:5-7*
    - *Jeremiah 22:3*
    - *Psalm 8*
    - *Psalm 139*
    - *Proverbs 6:16-19*
    - *Matthew 5:21-22*

_____

_____

_____

_____

13. Spend some time praying for your family and for your nation that we all might have a godly respect for human life.

CHAPTER TEN
TERROR HIGH

"'One of the most dangerous terrorist threats that America faces . . . [is] an al Qaeda operative born and raised in the United States, trained and committed to carry out deadly attacks on American soil.'"

U. S. Justice Department lawyers describing Ahmed Ali
(*Inside the Revolution*, page 135)

1. Who was Ahmed Ali and why was he dangerous? What did you find most interesting about his story?

   _____

   _____

   _____

2. Do you agree that many Americans "simply have no idea how aggressively Radicals are trying to infiltrate the United States, recruit Americans into terrorist cell groups, and gather the weaponry they need to pull off catastrophic attacks inside this country" (p. 133)? Why or why not?

   _____

   _____

3. What is your opinion of the work of the U.S. Department of Homeland Security after reading this chapter? Are they doing a good job? What could they be doing better?

4. Discuss the nature of Wahhabi Islam and why the West needs to be concerned about it.

5. Were you aware of the existence of the Islamic Saudi Academy (ISA) and other schools like it? What do you think about schools like ISA being allowed to exist in the United States?

6. How should we handle the tension between free speech and freedom of religion—both rights protected by the U.S. Constitution—and the need for society to protect itself from terrorism?

7. Based on the data presented in this chapter, how many Muslims are there in America?

8. Do you personally know any Muslims? What is your relationship with them like?

9. How many Radicals are there in the United States?

10. How many Radicals are there in Europe?

11. Do you believe it is inevitable or unavoidable that the U.S. and Great Britain will one day be living under Sharia law? Why or why not?

12. How many Radicals are there worldwide?

13. Review the demographic information about Muslims in America (pp. 46–47 of this study guide). What information, if any, was new to you? Were there any surprises?

___

14. Did you notice that 41 percent of Muslims in America say they pray five times a day? What is your prayer life like? How often do you stop and talk to God? What are you praying for?

___

15. What are some ways you and your family and friends could be praying for Muslims in America generally, and for any Muslims you know personally in particular?

___

16. Take some time now to pray.

_____

_____

_____

MUSLIMS IN AMERICA

U.S. citizens?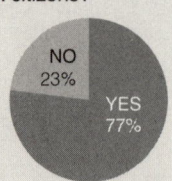

Born overseas?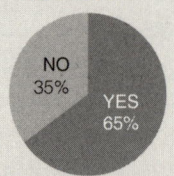

Age?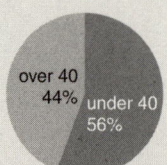

21% of Muslims in America are converts
59% of converts are African-Americans
34% are white
7% other
55% of converts become Sunnis
6% of converts become Shias
49% converted before the age of twenty-one
34% between ages of twenty-one and thirty-five
only 17% of converts are thirty-six or older

Of all foreign-born Muslims in the U.S.:
24% are from Arab countries
8% are from Iran
8% are from Pakistan
4% from India
3% from Bangladesh
the rest are from a range of other countries

Why did they come?
- 26% of foreign-born Muslims say they came to the U.S. for educational opportunities
- 24% for economic opportunities
- 24% for family reasons
- 20% because of conflict or persecution

What kind of Muslims?
- 50% of Muslims in America say they are Sunnis
- 16% say they are Shias
- 22% say they have no affiliation
- the rest were a potpourri of other traditions, or would not say

- 53% say it has gotten harder to be a Muslim in the U.S. since 9/11
- 25% say they have been personally discriminated against in the U.S.
- 73% they have suffered no discrimination in the U.S.

How devout?
- 41% pray five times a day
- 40% attend mosque once a week or more
- 26% go less than once a week
- 34% never go
- 77% of Iranian Muslims never go to mosque—only 7% go once a week
- 57% of Pakistani Muslims go to mosque more than once a week—14% never go

How political?
- 63% are Democrats or lean Democratic (71% voted for Kerry in 2004)
- 11% are Republican or lean Republican (only 14% voted for Bush in 2004)
- 26% are independents
- 43% believe mosques should express political views, while 49% say they should stay out of political issues

Source: Andrew Kohut, "Muslims in America: Middle Class and Mostly Mainstream," Pew Research Center, May 22, 2007

17. In this chapter, we see in even more detail how Radicals are investing in the training of young people to change the world. Read Deuteronomy 6:5-7 and 2 Timothy 3:14-15. Clearly, the Bible—both Old and New Testaments—also places an extremely high value on parents and teachers investing in the lives of young people. How are you implementing such verses in the lives of your own children or grandchildren, or in the lives of other children you know?

_____

_____

_____

18. This chapter also raises the question of how followers of Jesus Christ should treat people from other countries and cultures who are living among us. Spend some time looking up the following passages. How does the Bible teach us to care for foreigners and strangers?

    - *Deuteronomy 10:17-19*
    - *Hebrews 13:1-2*

_____

_____

_____

CHAPTER ELEVEN
REVOLUTION 2.0

"'Is it possible for us to witness a world without America and Zionism? You had best know that this slogan and this goal are attainable, and surely can be achieved.'"

Mahmoud Ahmadinejad (*Inside the Revolution*, pages 168–169)

1. How might Mahmoud Ahmadinejad's upbringing and early years have contributed to what he became as an adult? What were the strongest influences in his life?

   _____

   _____

   _____

2. What does it mean that Ahmadinejad's campaign rhetoric was "a potent and provocative cocktail of fundamentalist religion mixed with a dash of revolutionary Marxism" (p. 165)? Why would this approach have appealed to a lot of Iranians?

   _____

   _____

   _____

3. How do you explain that "almost no one in the West was watching closely or listening carefully" to what Ahmadinejad was threatening (p. 170)?

4. How did Ahmadinejad's beliefs in the coming of the Islamic messiah known as the Mahdi influence his campaigns for public office?

5. How did his beliefs in the coming of the Mahdi influence how he governed once in public office?

6. When I suggest that Ahmadinejad sees himself as a Shia Islamic version of John the Baptist, what does that mean?

7. Read the story of John the Baptist, beginning in Luke 1:5-25 and 1:57-80. Also read Luke 3:1-16. How did God set John apart for ministry? What was John's God-given mission?

8. Ayatollah Khomeini had planned very carefully to carry his revolution into the future by investing in well-selected disciples. On page 153, Ali Khamenei is described as a "bright and eloquent" young man. On page 161, Mahmoud Ahmadinejad is described as having "a powerful intellect and deep religious convictions." How has the Revolution Khomeini set in motion been furthered by his focus on discipleship?

9. The leaders of Babylon during the days of the Hebrew prophet Daniel knew the power of young people when they selected certain youths to educate for future leadership in their kingdom. Read Daniel 1. In what ways were these young men selected and educated?

10. Pray for a generation of young people to be raised up, trained in righteousness and grace, and ready to serve Jesus Christ in our world. What might be your part in recruiting, supporting, and training such godly young leaders?

_____

_____

_____

_____

CHAPTER TWELVE

MAKING WAY FOR THE MAHDI

"Not a single Western reporter who has interviewed Ahmadinejad—one of the most dangerous men in the world— has ever asked him directly about his eschatology."
Inside the Revolution, page 172

1. What does it mean that Ahmadinejad launched a "charm offensive" during a visit to the United States (p. 171)?

   _____

   _____

   _____

2. Why do you think no major American journalists asked Ahmadinejad about his Shia religious beliefs while he was in the United States? How does this coverage differ from how American politicians are quizzed about their religious beliefs?

   _____

   _____

   _____

3. Summarize the Shia Muslim vision of the End Times. Who is the Mahdi and what is he supposed to do?

4. Why should the End Times beliefs of Iranian leaders matter to the West?

5. Secretary of State Hillary Clinton once suggested that if Iran strikes first, the United States should strike back. What are the pros and cons of this approach in light of the End Times beliefs of Iranian leaders?

6. Do you believe we can live with an Iran that has acquired nuclear weapons? Why or why not?

_____

_____

_____

_____

7. What should the U.S. and our allies be doing to stop Iran's bid for nuclear weapons?

_____

_____

_____

_____

8. Can Iran be deterred and contained if it is led by men who believe it is their God-given mission to bring about the end of the world?

_____

_____

_____

_____

9. As Iranian leaders prepare and proclaim the end of the world and the coming of their Islamic "messiah," their focus is very clear. Are you focused on being prepared for Jesus' return? How should you live differently if you really believe time is short?

10. Look up Ephesians 5:15-21. How does the Bible tells us to live in evil days?

11. Read 2 Peter 3. What do we learn in this passage about how to live in the "last days" before the return of Jesus?

12. How are you doing right now in your walk with Jesus Christ? Are you living a holy and pure life? If not, read 1 John 1:9. Confess your sins and ask Christ to forgive you and cleanse you from all unrighteousness. Ask Him to fill you with the Holy Spirit and teach you to live a life worthy of Him before He comes back to earth.

CHAPTER THIRTEEN
THE ROAD AHEAD

"How dare the world keep silent about what is being done by Radicals in the name of God? Silence betrays and dishonors the memories of the innocents who were killed without cause."
Inside the Revolution, page 195

1. What factor makes the jihadist threat different and more dangerous than other historic threats to national security?

   _____

   _____

   _____

   _____

2. What does this particularly heinous tactic say about the Radicals' respect for the sanctity of life?

   _____

   _____

   _____

3. How does having an open society in the United States leave us vulnerable to terrorist attacks? In what ways does our society seemingly contribute to its own downfall?

___

___

___

4. Why do you think we haven't caught bin Laden yet?

___

___

___

5. Review Porter Goss's list of the seven biggest threats to Western society (pp. 198–211). Which of these threats do you think loom largest?

___

___

___

6. What are some signs of hope in Iran, according to Goss?

___

___

___

7. What is "economic jihad," and how have the Radicals been trying to sabotage Western economies?

8. What steps should the West in general and the United States in particular be taking to achieve energy independence in light of the geopolitical volatility in the epicenter?

9. As we finish this section on the Radicals, take some time to read through Psalm 71. Humanly speaking, the road ahead is filled with threats and dangers and thus can be discouraging. But ask the Lord to be Your strength, and take some time to pray for protection and hope as the psalmist does.

10. Read Philippians 4:4-9. How does the apostle Paul tell us to live in the light that "the Lord is near"? How is it possible to rejoice always, even when we face grave dangers?

11. If you have a study Bible, take a look at the introduction to Philippians. Where was Paul writing this letter from? Was he living a life of safety and comfort as he drafted this epistle to the church at Philippi?

_____

_____

_____

12. Paul tells us not to be fixated on evil. What does he tell us to fix our minds upon?

_____

_____

_____

13. If you know people who are worried about the future, share the Philippians passage with them. Remember, too, the Proverbs 31 woman who "smiles at the future" (literally, "the latter days"). May we be like her.

the REFORMERS
PART TWO

CHAPTER FOURTEEN

"ISLAM IS THE ANSWER, BUT JIHAD IS NOT THE WAY"

"The mainstream media has, frankly, done a terrible job examining the internal tensions and enormous diversity of beliefs and practices within the Muslim world."
Inside the Revolution, page 215

1. Who are the Reformers? What do they want? How do they differ from the Radicals?

   _____

   _____

   _____

   _____

2. Explain what is meant by "Jeffersonian democracy." What do the Reformers have to do with Thomas Jefferson?

   _____

   _____

   _____

3. Who are some of the key Reformers in the epicenter?

4. Discuss some of the Reformer successes in the Middle East. What lessons can be learned from these successes?

5. Do you agree that we don't hear much in the news about these successes? If so, why do you think that is, and what can be done about it?

6. Most of the Reformers in the Middle East believe that God exists and is actively involved in the affairs of men. The leaders of the American Revolution believed this as well. On page 218, I quote Thomas Jefferson calling the Lord the "Infinite Power which rules the destinies of the universe." Do you believe that? If so, why is it important to democracy to believe that God—not the state—is ultimately in charge of our destinies?

_____

_____

_____

7. If God endows the men and women He created with certain unalienable rights—among them, the right to life, liberty, and the pursuit of happiness—what then is the role of the government?

_____

_____

_____

8. Read Daniel 2:20-22. List the powers that the God of the Bible has. Can a leader rise to power without God's permission or approval?

_____

_____

_____

9. We know the Lord has brought these various Reformer leaders to power. Spend some time thanking the Lord for them, praying for their peace and wisdom as they seek to lead their countries wisely.

10. Make a list of the five "snapshot" countries listed here and pray for each one by name. Make it your plan to research for yourself what is happening in these five countries and pray knowledgeably for them.

_____

_____

_____

_____

CHAPTER FIFTEEN
THE THEOLOGY OF THE REFORMERS

"'To say Islam is peaceful? It is not. But it can be taught peacefully. The [Qur'an] texts allow you to do this.'"
Tawfik Hamid, a former Islamic Radical who is now a Reformer
(*Inside the Revolution*, page 234)

1. Why do Reformers argue that Islam is a peaceful religion? What verses in the Qur'an do they point to?

   _____

   _____

   _____

2. What are some of the points of disagreement between Reformers and Radicals, and even between different Radical factions?

   _____

   _____

   _____

   _____

3. Review the story of Benazir Bhutto (pp. 227–230). In what ways did she exhibit the characteristics of a Reformer?

4. Why did the Radicals hate Bhutto?

5. Why did Reformers resent her?

6. What actions did Bhutto take to deal with the criticisms directed at her? What was the outcome?

7. Would you consider Bhutto an effective leader? Why or why not?

8. What was contained in Sayyed Imam al-Sharif's manifesto? What could this mean for the future of Muslim countries?

9. Benazir Bhutto's book was titled, *Reconciliation: Islam, Democracy, and the West.* Read 2 Corinthians 5:17-20. What does the apostle Paul say about how mankind is reconciled to God?

10. Read Ephesians 2:13-18. How do we find peace with God? How do we find peace and reconciliation with other men and women who are our enemies?

_____

_____

_____

11. Spend some time praying that Reformers will find peace and reconciliation.

12. Pray that more and more influential leaders would become true peacemakers.

CHAPTER SIXTEEN
THE DEFECTOR

"Iran will gain real power if freedom and democracy develop there. Strength will not be obtained through weapons and the Bomb."

Hossein Khomeini (*Inside the Revolution*, page 242)

1. Who is Hossein Khomeini, and what did he do that made headlines?

   _____

   _____

   _____

   _____

2. How did he arrive at the decision to do what he did?

   _____

   _____

   _____

   _____

3. How does the Muslim world react to such defectors?

4. Who are "the despondent" in Iran today, and why are they using so many drugs?

5. Who are "the disgusted" in Iran today, and what crimes of the government do they point to?

6. Is such despair and anger unique to Iran? What do you think is happening throughout the Muslim world?

7. How do such social conditions create an opening for the Reformers to make their case for a different approach?

8. Hossein Khomeini referred to "a religious government" being established only "after the reappearance of the absent [Twelfth] Imam." The Bible, of course, indicates clearly that Jesus is the Messiah and that He will come back to earth to establish His kingdom. Read Isaiah 9:6-7. What do we learn about the biblical Messiah's reign on earth?

9. Read Isaiah 11:6-9. What changes in nature will we see when the Messiah reigns over all the earth?

10. Read Luke 1:30-33. What was Jesus' mission when He came to earth?

11. Read Revelation 20:1-6. According to this passage, how long will Jesus Christ and His followers reign on earth in the last days before heaven and earth are destroyed?

12. Read Revelation 20:10-15 and Revelation 21–22. What do we learn about how Jesus will set up His ultimate and eternal kingdom on the new earth after Satan and his angels are cast into the lake of fire?

13. The population of Iran is suffering in so many ways, as described in this chapter. Spend some time praying Psalm 30 for the Iranian people, that the Lord will turn their "mourning into dancing" even before He establishes His earthly kingdom.

CHAPTER SEVENTEEN
MEET HAMID KARZAI

"If the world had done more, the Twin Towers would be standing today."

Hamid Karzai (*Inside the Revolution*, page 261)

1. Who is Hamid Karzai? What did he achieve? How did he do it?

   _____

   _____

   _____

   _____

   _____

2. Describe the situation in Afghanistan before Karzai took office.

   _____

   _____

   _____

   _____

3. Do you see any ways in which Karzai's youth and upbringing contributed to his adult achievements?

_____

_____

_____

4. Do you agree with Karzai that the world should have done more to stop the Taliban and al Qaeda before 9/11? What should the U.S. have done? Would you have supported aggressive, relentless military strikes against al Qaeda and the Taliban—even the introduction of ground troops in Afghanistan and "regime change" in Kabul—before the 9/11 attacks?

_____

_____

_____

_____

5. The story of Afghanistan is partly a story of the Soviet Union raping and pillaging that nation and the United States initially helping to liberate the country but then abandoning the Afghan people after the Soviets withdrew. Aside from the role of nations, what is the responsibility of individual followers of Jesus seeking to build His kingdom in caring for suffering people?

_____

_____

6. Read Matthew 25:31-46. List the responsibilities that Jesus mentions here regarding the expectations He has for His followers.

7. Read Luke 4:14-21. In this passage, Jesus quotes Isaiah 61:1-2. What does He say His mission—the mission of the Messiah—includes?

8. Pray for the Lord to raise up more workers to serve the poor, the needy, and the suffering in difficult and dangerous places. What might be your role in bringing relief to those who are suffering?

CHAPTER EIGHTEEN
KARZAI'S MISSION

"'How can you have justice if you don't have people voting and choosing their governments?'"
Hamid Karzai (*Inside the Revolution*, page 266)

1. What are some of the reforms that Karzai has achieved since being in office?

   _____

   _____

   _____

2. Why are some saying that Karzai is a puppet of the West? What is your opinion of that accusation?

   _____

   _____

   _____

   _____

3. Discuss the qualities that Karzai seems to have in common with Thomas Jefferson. How are these the qualities of a good leader?

4. Are you hopeful about the future of Afghanistan? What more should the West be doing there to strengthen the hand of the Reformers?

5. Hamid Karzai's story illustrates the importance of wise and trustworthy leadership. How does the Bible describe a godly leader? Note your insights from the following verses:

- *Deuteronomy 17:15-20*
- *2 Samuel 23:1-4*
- *Psalm 1*
- *Proverbs 24:5-6*
- *Proverbs 29:1-14*

6. Read 1 Timothy 2:1-2. How does the apostle Paul instruct us to intercede for our leaders?

_____

_____

_____

7. Spend some time praying for the leaders of your country and those around the world who are making decisions for their people. Ask for God's will to be done and His Word to spread far and near. Use the verses you studied to pray for godly leaders.

8. Create a list of leaders in the Middle East and begin to pray for them by name. Think of the influence you can have on these leaders by interceding for them before the Lord on your knees.

_____

_____

_____

_____

_____

CHAPTER NINETEEN
"WE ARE FIGHTING ISLAMIC FASCISTS"

"'Iraq will not forget those who stood with her and who continue to stand with her in times of need.'"
Nouri al-Maliki (*Inside the Revolution*, page 281)

1. Who is Nouri al-Maliki? What has he achieved? How has he done it?

_____

_____

_____

_____

2. What did Maliki's speech demonstrate about the U.S. troops serving in Iraq?

_____

_____

_____

3. What criticism did Maliki receive from various American leaders? Why?

4. How did Maliki respond?

5. Why were many Americans opposed to the war in Iraq?

6. What progress has been made in Iraq?

7. Prime Minister Maliki is quoted on page 283 saying, "God has made us free." What does the Bible have to say about freedom?

    - *John 8:31-36*
    - *Galatians 5:13-14*
    - *1 Peter 2:12-17*

    _____

    _____

    _____

    _____

8. Spend some time praying for the Lord to shine His freedom and justice into every dark corner of Iraq and the rest of the Muslim world.

CHAPTER TWENTY
MEET JALAL TALABANI

"We will spare no effort to present Iraq as a model of democracy."
Jalal Talabani (*Inside the Revolution*, page 309)

1. Who is Jalal Talabani? How did he get to the position he holds?

   _____

   _____

   _____

   _____

2. Who are the Kurdish people?

   _____

   _____

   _____

   _____

3. How did they suffer under Saddam Hussein?

　

4. How did Talabani contribute to the fall of Saddam Hussein?

　

5. In what ways is Talabani a Reformer?

　

6. In the Bible, the Kurdish people are known as the Medes, part of the Media-Persian empire. A careful study of the Scriptures makes it clear that God has a great love for the Kurds and wants them to know Him personally. Read Acts 2:9. List in order the people groups present in Jerusalem when the apostle

Peter preached the gospel of Jesus Christ for the first time on the Day of Pentecost. Where do the Medes fall in the list?

7. Read Daniel 5:31 and all of chapter 6. What remarkable things did God do through the Hebrew prophet Daniel to reveal Himself to King Darius, who was a Mede?

8. Read Jeremiah 51:11 and 51:28-29. How will God use the Medes/Kurds to fulfill the judgment of Babylon in the last days?

CHAPTER TWENTY-ONE
TALABANI'S TEST

"'We are proud to say openly and to repeat it, that we are partners of the United States of America in fighting against tyranny, terrorism, and for democracy.'"
Jalal Talabani (*Inside the Revolution*, page 312)

1. How has Jalal Talabani been tested since becoming president of Iraq?

2. What was the Bush-McCain surge policy?

3. Why was it so bitterly opposed by some U.S. leaders, including then senators Barack Obama and Hillary Clinton?

_____

_____

_____

_____

4. What have been President Talabani's fears about U.S. and Coalition forces pulling out of Iraq too early? What would be the worst-case scenario?

_____

_____

_____

_____

5. Do you agree with the statements made by then senators Barack Obama and Joe Biden, along with others, that encouraging freedom and democracy in Iraq is "naive" and even "ridiculous"? Why or why not?

_____

_____

_____

_____

6. What has been the outcome of the surge?

_____
_____
_____
_____

7. Do you now see signs of hope for Iraqi democracy and security where it once looked hopeless? Why or why not?

_____
_____
_____
_____

8. Who is Qubad Talabani? What points struck you as significant from my interview with him?

_____
_____
_____
_____

9. Were you aware of the growing religious freedom in Iraq, particularly for Christians? Why is this significant?

_____

_____

_____

10. These chapters have described the increasing stability and success of the northern Iraqi territories of Kurdistan. Some, such as Jalal and Qubad Talabani, are hopeful that this model can be replicated in all of Iraq. Others are skeptical. What does the Bible say about the future of Iraq?

_____

_____

_____

11. In the Bible, the region we know today as Iraq is known as Babel, Babylon, Babylonia, Mesopotamia, Chaldea, and Shinar. The Scriptures also make clear that the ancient city of Babylon—once the wealthiest and most powerful on the planet—will be rebuilt in the last days. Read Revelation 18. What do we learn about how phenomenally wealthy Babylon will become?

_____

_____

_____

12. Can Iraq the country and Babylon the city be fully rebuilt and become so wealthy unless there is peace? What, then, should we expect to see happen in Iraq in the years ahead?

_____

_____

_____

_____

13. Though Iraq and Babylon become the epicenter of wealth and power in the last days, what does Revelation 18 tell us about the spiritual condition of the people at that time?

_____

_____

_____

_____

14. What does Revelation 18 tell us about the judgment God will eventually inflict upon Iraq/Babylon in the last days?

_____

_____

_____

_____

15. Read Jeremiah 50–51. What additional details do we learn about how powerful Iraq/Babylon will be in the last days? What more do we learn about the judgment coming to Babylon?

_____

_____

_____

_____

16. In light of the fact that the Bible says Iraq/Babylon will have great success and horrific failure in the last days, take some time now to pray for the people of Iraq and for the gospel of Jesus Christ to be spread to each and every person there while there is still time.

CHAPTER TWENTY-TWO
THE KING AND I

"'There is an Arab proverb that says, "Don't be a mute Satan." I feel compelled to do everything I can to make a better world.'"
Dr. Ahmed Abaddi (*Inside the Revolution*, page 335)

1. Who is Dr. Ahmed Abaddi and why is he significant among Muslims?

___

___

___

___

2. Who is Mohammed VI, and why does Abaddi call him "one of the boldest Reformers in the Muslim world" (p. 333)?

___

___

___

___

3. What are Mohammed VI's hopes and dreams for Morocco and its Muslim neighbors?

4. Have you ever traveled to a Muslim country? If so, where? What were your impressions? If not, and money were no object, would you ever go to a Muslim country? Why or why not?

5. The Moroccans are blessed to have men of peace leading them. In the Scriptures, Jesus sent His disciples out to preach the Kingdom of Heaven. What instructions did Jesus give in Luke 10:1-11 regarding encounters with a "man of peace"?

6. How can these instructions apply today in terms of interacting with Reformers?

_____

_____

_____

_____

7. In Acts 10, a man named Cornelius is described. Read the story of Peter and Cornelius and write down the characteristics of Cornelius.

_____

_____

_____

_____

8. What did the Lord instruct Peter to do with regard to meeting a person who was not yet a follower of Jesus Christ but wanted to follow God and had a proven track record of being a man of peace?

_____

_____

_____

_____

9. Read Psalm 37:37 and Isaiah 32:16-18. Use these verses to pray for the peace of Morocco—that righteousness would shine forth from that country.

CHAPTER TWENTY-THREE
THE MOROCCAN MODEL

"Today, Moroccans enjoy far more freedom to say what they want, write what they want, and organize their political parties, labor unions, human-rights organizations, and social reform groups than they did under the current king's father—and far more than almost anywhere in the Islamic world."
Inside the Revolution, page 352

1. What do you think of King Mohammed VI's twelve-step plan "to battle the Radicals and spread Morocco's message of reform" (p. 341)?

   _____

   _____

   _____

   _____

2. Dr. Abaddi lists the Radicals' most pressing complaints as (1) Europe's past colonization of Muslim countries; (2) the West's exploitation of the region's natural resources; (3) the polluting influence of Hollywood movies; (4) an alleged historic conspiracy in the West against the Ottoman Empire; (5) the West's friendship toward Israel; and (6) the very

existence of Israel. To what extent do you agree that these complaints have merit, if any? What are some other ways they might be addressed without the use of violent jihad?

3. What do you think of Morocco's intention to train a new generation of moderate Islamic preachers and scholars? What kind of impact do you think this would have on the waging of jihad? Why?

4. Consider the king's efforts to reach out to evangelical Christians. What are some possible results of such a "bridge of friendship"?

5. Discuss how the empowerment of women, the easing of poverty, and the adoption of democratic ideals might contribute to a more peaceful Morocco. Might such measures invite scorn or even retaliation from Radical Muslims? Is this a risk Morocco is willing to take? Why?

_____

_____

_____

6. On page 359, Dr. Abaddi says he feels evangelical Christians are "gentlemen" who can be trusted. "We are trying to reach out to the real America. Evangelicals are serious people, helpful people." Why is it so important for followers of Jesus to be truly honorable, honest, helpful people?

_____

_____

_____

_____

7. Read John 13:34-35. According to Jesus, how will people know that you are His follower?

_____

_____

_____

8. Read Matthew 5:1-16. List the characteristics that a godly and winsome follower of Jesus Christ will possess.

_____

_____

_____

9. How do people perceive you? Do unbelievers know you are a follower of Jesus Christ because you demonstrate extraordinary, Christlike love for them and for others? How can you improve in this area?

_____

_____

_____

10. What are some ways you can do a better job letting your light shine before men that they may "glorify your Father who is in heaven"?

_____

_____

_____

the REVIVALISTS

PART THREE

CHAPTER TWENTY-FOUR
"ISLAM IS NOT THE ANSWER, AND JIHAD IS NOT THE WAY; JESUS IS THE WAY"

"'I was a Palestinian sniper. But then I fell in love with a Savior who loves Arabs as well as Jews.'"
Tass Saada (*Inside the Revolution*, page 365)

1. Before reading *Inside the Revolution*, did you realize that so many Muslims are coming to Christ? If so, where had you heard about it? If not, why do you think it's not bigger news?

   _____

   _____

   _____

   _____

2. What is the definition of a Revivalist?

   _____

   _____

   _____

3. What is the Revivalists' goal?

4. Discuss the two groups of Revivalists: Muslim Background Believers (MBBs) and Nominal Christian Background Believers (NCBBs). What are the challenges faced by each group?

5. Does being born into a Muslim family make you a Muslim? Explain.

6. Read John 1:12; 3:3; 14:6; Romans 10:9-10; 2 Corinthians 5:17-18. Does being born into a Christian family make you a Christian? How does that differ from the Muslim view?

7. How do Revivalists differ from Radicals and Reformers?

8. What, if anything, do Revivalists have in common with those groups?

9. Explain the differences between a Radical's idea of personal sacrifice and a Revivalist's idea of personal sacrifice.

___

10. What are your reactions to the story of Tass Saada, his background, and how he came to know Christ? Do you see similarities between Tass's story and that of the apostle Paul? What does Tass's story demonstrate about the nature of God?

___

11. Share your response to my question, "What role does the Lord have for *us* [believers] in strengthening our brothers and sisters who come to Christ from a Muslim background, and how can we actively love our neighbors and our enemies when, humanly speaking, this is impossible?" (p. 367).

12. It is thrilling to read the stories of people's lives being transformed by the love of Jesus Christ. Read the story of the apostle Paul's conversion to Christ in Acts 9:1-31. Describe the contrast between who "Saul" was and who "Paul" became—the before and after story.

13. Read Colossians 3. List what happens when a person's life is transformed by faith in Jesus Christ.

CHAPTER TWENTY-FIVE
THE BIG, UNTOLD STORY—PART ONE

"'In the last 20 years, more Iranians have come to Christ [than in] the last 14 centuries.'"
Lazarus Yeghnazar, Iranian-born evangelist (*Inside the Revolution*, page 384)

1. What are some of the reasons for Muslims turning to Christ? What is attractive to them about the Christian faith?

   _____

   _____

   _____

   _____

2. What unique challenges are Revivalists up against?

   _____

   _____

   _____

   _____

3. Read Matthew 28:18-20 and Acts 1:6-8. What are their sources of strength and encouragement?

4. One Iranian Christian quoted in the book said that in his country, "you don't go after people with the gospel. They are coming to you to ask you about the Lord" (p. 383). Why do you think that is? What would it take for North Americans and Europeans to exhibit the same sort of eagerness for the gospel?

5. Discuss the paradox of how harsh persecution of Christianity, such as that in Iran under the ayatollahs and Ahmadinejad, so often results in the dramatic growth of the Church.

6. What do you think about the Lord's use of dreams and visions to draw Muslims to Himself? Why might these kinds of

experiences be more common (or more commonly reported) in the Middle East than in Western countries?

_____

_____

_____

7. Read Joel 2:28-32. Do you believe we are seeing these verses fulfilled in our lifetime? Why or why not?

_____

_____

_____

8. How does Paul describe his coming to faith in Christ in Galatians 1:12?

_____

_____

_____

9. So many people are disillusioned, discouraged, and seeking for peace and hope in the Middle East. What can we learn in Matthew 7:7-11 about God's attitude toward those who seek Him?

_____

_____

_____

10. It is not easy to bring the good news of Jesus Christ to the Middle East. There are legitimate reasons for fear. Yet what is Paul's instruction to Christ-followers in 2 Timothy 1:7-12? On what basis did Paul find courage to serve Jesus in the epicenter?

_____

_____

_____

_____

11. What does the Bible say about those who are persecuted and suffer for Christ's sake?

    - *Matthew 5:10-16*
    - *1 Corinthians 4:9-16*
    - *2 Corinthians 4:5-18*
    - *2 Timothy 3:12*

_____

_____

_____

_____

12. Take time to pray for the persecuted church. It is our duty to remember those who are in prison and persecuted for their faith in Jesus Christ (see 1 Corinthians 12:26).

CHAPTER TWENTY-SIX
THE BIG, UNTOLD STORY— PART TWO

"'What! You made us wait five days to hear about Jesus?'"
Father of a Moroccan Christian who had been reluctant to share her faith
(*Inside the Revolution*, page 392)

1. Share your thoughts about Cairo's "garbage church." In what ways is it similar to or different from the typical contemporary church in America?

   _____
   _____
   _____
   _____

2. What accounts for the dramatic spiritual awakening under way in Iraq?

   _____
   _____
   _____
   _____

3. In some Muslim countries, like Syria, women "are particularly receptive to the gospel" (p. 397). What might be some possible reasons for this?

_____

_____

_____

_____

4. As you read through the testimonies of believers in countries like Lebanon, Syria, Afghanistan, Pakistan, and Saudi Arabia, are there any common patterns that you observe? What are they?

_____

_____

_____

5. The Coptic priest who started the "garbage church" in Cairo referred to being the "scum of the world." Read 1 Corinthians 4:13; what do you think of the priest's statement in light of what Paul says in this verse?

_____

_____

_____

_____

6. Read Luke 14:7-24. Jesus shared two parables with guests at an elaborate dinner party. What do you learn from these parables? How do these parables apply to reaching people for the gospel in poor regions of the Muslim world?

_____

_____

_____

7. What is Jesus' reaction to those who are needy? Read the following and make note of Jesus' heart and actions.

   - *Matthew 9:35-38*
   - *Matthew 20:29-34*
   - *Luke 7:12-17*

_____

_____

_____

8. It can be intimidating to look at a Muslim religious leader or a Muslim political leader or a Muslim woman who is fully veiled; you may think, "This person doesn't want to learn about Jesus." But what is the perspective of God in 1 Samuel 16:7?

_____

_____

_____

9. This chapter describes the exciting revivals going on in many countries of the Muslim world. What is the definition of a revival? How can this term be applied to these countries?

_____

_____

_____

10. Read the following verses and note what you learn about revival. What are the causes of revival?

    - *Hosea 10:12*
    - *2 Chronicles 7:14*
    - *Psalm 119:25, 37, 40, 88, 107, 149, 153-160*

_____

_____

_____

11. Pray that the Lord will continue to pour out His Holy Spirit on the countries of the Muslim world and that many millions of people will find hope and peace in Jesus Christ.

CHAPTER TWENTY-SEVEN
THE AIR WAR

"For Muslims who are curious about Christianity but equally fearful of anyone knowing about their interest, [satellite broadcast] services give them a safe window into a world of ideas to which they feel increasingly drawn."
Inside the Revolution, page 417

1. What do I mean by *air war* in this chapter?

   _____

   _____

   _____

2. What factors make the twenty-first century a particularly good time to launch a spiritual air war in the Middle East?

   _____

   _____

   _____

   _____

3. What is the goal of Revivalist air warriors, and why are they so hated by certain Muslim factions? Do you think they are achieving their aims?

_____

_____

_____

_____

4. Consider the approach Father Zakaria Botros takes to get listeners' attention and lead them to Christ, including his "top ten" list of what Muslims would need to do to stop him. Do you think he's got the right approach? Why or why not?

_____

_____

_____

_____

5. What makes Hormoz Shariat the "Billy Graham of Iran" (p. 417)?

_____

_____

_____

_____

6. This air war that I describe is communicating God's Word in the places on earth where it is very difficult to penetrate by land. Though it is impossible to personally follow up the millions who listen and watch the various radio and television programs, how can we be assured that God's Word is having an effect on the audience? Read the following verses and write down how we can be confident in the eternal impact of God's Word:

   - *Hebrews 4:12-13*
   - *2 Timothy 3:14-17*
   - *Isaiah 55:10-13*

   _____
   _____
   _____
   _____

7. Jesus tells the parable of the sower and the seed in Matthew 13:1-23. Read this parable and describe the different types of soil mentioned. What do they represent? What does the seed represent?

   _____
   _____
   _____
   _____

8. Spend some time praying for the Lord to prepare the soil of people's hearts in the Muslim world, so that when they hear the seed of God's Word it will bear much fruit.

9. How can we be praying for those engaged in the air war? How else can we help them?

_____

_____

_____

_____

10. Take some time to pray now for those engaged in radio, TV, and Internet ministry in the epicenter.

CHAPTER TWENTY-EIGHT
THE GROUND WAR— PART ONE

"The key is the personal touch."
Inside the Revolution, page 427

1. What do I mean by *ground war* in this context? How does it differ from the air war in the previous chapter?

   _____

   _____

   _____

   _____

2. What do ground war Revivalists feel is the key to making disciples of their fellow Muslims? Why do they think this way? Who is their example?

   _____

   _____

   _____

   _____

3. In what ways might the typical Middle Eastern lifestyle be more conducive to a ground war approach to sharing the gospel than a typical Western lifestyle?

4. Read Ephesians 6:10-20. How does a Revivalist prepare for a day of spiritual warfare (see p. 429)? To what extent does this description sound like how you prepare for your day?

5. What is the true cost of discipleship among ground war Revivalists?

6. If spiritual awakening inevitably brings trouble, why pray for revival?

7. Read Luke 15:1-7. Here Jesus tells the parable of the lost sheep. Think for a moment about the danger the shepherd incurs by searching for his one lost sheep. Why would he risk it?

8. We discussed the danger of taking the gospel into the Muslim world via a ground war approach. It is understandable that few are willing to go. But how did Jesus instruct us to pray in Matthew 9:35-38? Why is it so urgent that we not be immobilized by fear, given the enormous opportunities that lie before us?

9. Spend some time praying for those men, women, and children who put their very lives on the line to bring hope through Jesus Christ to Muslims without any hope. Read and pray through these verses on their behalf:

   - *Deuteronomy 31:6*
   - *2 Chronicles 15:4-6*
   - *Acts 23:11*
   - *Galatians 6:9*

CHAPTER TWENTY-NINE
THE GROUND WAR— PART TWO

"He called me to follow Him alone. He made it clear that He had a very big work to do and that He was calling me to be part of it."
Samir, former Shiite seminary professor, now a Christian
(*Inside the Revolution,* page 440)

1. What does the Qur'an teach about Jesus? What does it get right? Where does it fall short of a full description?

   _____

   _____

   _____

   _____

2. Discuss the story of Samir and how he came to know and love the Lord. What means did God use to reach him?

   _____

   _____

   _____

3. Compare Samir's story to the story of Kerem. How did God draw Kerem to Himself?

4. Kerem, whose story we read in this chapter, was deeply affected by the Sermon on the Mount. Read Jesus' words in Matthew 5–7 and describe what might have been especially appealing to Kerem.

5. How does Jesus teach us to treat our enemies?

6. Kerem read several verses that convinced him to get baptized after converting from Islam to Christianity. Read these verses and, if you have never been baptized as a believer in Jesus Christ, seriously consider following Jesus' example of obedience through baptism.

   - *Matthew 3:2*
   - *Matthew 3:13-17*
   - *Matthew 28:18-20*

7. Read Romans 10:8-17. Describe our responsibility to share the gospel. Even though so many are coming to Christ through dreams and visions, what is the reason to continue risking lives to bring the gospel to everyone in the epicenter in person?

   _____

   _____

   _____

   _____

8. Philemon 1:6 in the New International Version of the Bible says, "I pray that you may be active in sharing your faith, so that you will have a full understanding of every good thing we have in Christ." How active are you in sharing your faith in Jesus Christ with courage? Have you ever had such an opportunity?

   _____

   _____

   _____

9. If you have never been trained in sharing your faith, take some time to ask the Lord to show you where and how you can get such training through your church or through some other evangelical ministry.

10. Spend some time praying for these heroes of the faith who are obediently proclaiming the good news in dangerous places. Commit to getting to know some of these servants of Christ as individuals or families. Serve them in prayer, encouragement, hospitality, and every other way you can.

CHAPTER THIRTY
THE THEOLOGY OF THE REVIVALISTS

"I was mocked and persecuted by many. Once I was beaten by eight people. I was nearly assassinated three times. But it is okay. Since I came to know the Lord Jesus as my Savior, I am ready to put my life—and my family—as a sacrifice for Jesus."

Shakir, former jihadist cell commander, now a Christian
(*Inside the Revolution*, page 456)

1. Has God ever called you to "Nineveh"—a place you didn't want to go, for a task you didn't want to do? Discuss how you did—or didn't—respond.

   _____

   _____

   _____

2. Discuss the story of Shakir. How did he come to know the Lord? How is his story different from or similar to other accounts you've read in *Inside the Revolution*?

   _____

   _____

   _____

3. What are the five common core convictions of Revivalists (pp. 456–469)?

4. Do you personally believe God loves you and has a wonderful plan for your life? Why or why not? Why is this belief foremost in the minds of the Revivalists?

5. Do you believe you are sinful and separated from God? If God loves us, then why does He say the "wages of sin is death," or eternal separation from Him (Romans 6:23)?

6. Do you believe that hell is a real place? Jesus did. He talked more about hell than heaven. If He is right, what are the implications for you?

_____

_____

_____

7. Do you believe that Jesus died on the cross? Do you believe that He rose from the dead on the third day? How does Jesus' death solve our problem that we are all sinful, separated from God, and thus condemned to hell?

_____

_____

_____

_____

8. Have you ever individually received Jesus Christ as your personal Savior and Lord? If so, describe what you did and when you did it. How did your life change from that moment?

_____

_____

_____

_____

If you have never received Jesus Christ into your life to forgive your sins—or if you're just not sure—would you like to make that decision right now?
   Read the following passages from the Bible:

- *John 1:12*
- *Romans 10:9-10, 13, 17*
- *Ephesians 2:8-9*
- *Revelation 3:20*

Are you ready to make the decision to receive Jesus Christ as your Savior and Lord? Here is a suggested prayer that has been helpful to many Muslims, Jews, and others—including my father and me—in becoming followers of Christ. The key is not so much the precise words as the attitude of your heart.

> Lord Jesus, thank You for loving me. Thank You for having a wonderful plan and purpose for my life. I need You today—I need You to forgive me for all of my sins. Thank You for dying on the cross to pay the penalty for my sins. Thank You for rising again from the dead to prove that You are the Way, the Truth, and the Life and the only way to get to heaven. I open the door of my heart and my life right now. I receive You as my Savior and Lord. Thank You for forgiving my sins and giving me eternal life. Please change my life. Please fill me with your Holy Spirit. Please take control of my life and make me the kind of person that You want me to be, so that I can serve You and please You forever. Thank You so much. I love You, and I want to follow You. Amen.

If you have just prayed this prayer, congratulations! Take a moment to pray and thank the Lord for adopting you into His family and making you a new person. Then, take time to call some family members or friends to tell them the exciting decision you have just made and why you made it.

9. Take a moment to consider Core Conviction #5. Why are Christ-followers commanded to love their neighbors and their enemies and to make disciples of all nations?

_____

_____

_____

10. What verses in the Bible do the Revivalists base this on?

_____

_____

_____

11. How are you doing in terms of loving your neighbors, regardless of their religion?

_____

_____

_____

12. How are you doing in terms of loving your enemies?

_____

_____

_____

13. How does Jesus want you to live? What specific, concrete steps could you take to obey Jesus in these critical areas?

_____

_____

_____

_____

14. Once you've answered these questions, develop a list a verses to memorize. Also, develop a list of prayer needs that came up for your life as you read this chapter. Through Shakir's story we looked at the greatest message of hope in the world. Commit yourself, in prayer, to sharing this message with as many as you can!

CHAPTER THIRTY-ONE
MAKING WAY FOR THE MESSIAH

"Given how closely world events are tracking with Bible prophecy, [Revivalists] find themselves increasingly motivated to 'be ready' and 'be prepared' for His arrival."
Inside the Revolution, page 475

1. What does the term *eschatology* mean? Why should it matter to followers of Jesus Christ?

   _____

   _____

   _____

   _____

2. Discuss why Bible prophecy and current events are an increasingly hot topic worldwide.

   _____

   _____

   _____

3. Read 1 Thessalonians 4:16-17. What is the Rapture? Who will go to heaven to meet Jesus at that moment in history?

4. Read Revelation 19:11–20:6. What is the second coming of Christ? How long does the Bible say Jesus will reign as King on earth after He physically touches down on earth?

5. Do you believe we are living in what the Bible calls the last days? Why or why not?

6. Read Matthew 24. What did Jesus say when asked what to look for in the End Times? Make a list of specific signs to watch for.

_____

_____

_____

7. What is the parable of the fig tree Jesus refers to in Matthew 24:32-33?

_____

_____

_____

8. Not all Christians agree on End Times prophecy, but why do so many Revivalists sense the return of Jesus is drawing near?

_____

_____

_____

9. What role will the United States play in the End Times, if any?

_____

_____

_____

10. Is it possible that we will see the emergence of an actual figure that Shia Muslims will point to as the Mahdi? What did Jesus say that might be applicable to this question?

11. Read Ezekiel 36–37. What specific future events are described as happening? Do you believe that all or most of these prophecies have been fulfilled in the last hundred years? Why or why not?

12. Read Ezekiel 38–39. What are a few specific events that will happen after the rebirth of Israel in the "last days" (38:16)?

13. What are the implications of biblical End Times prophecy for the Middle East, particularly for Iran and Israel?

14. Will any good come out of the War of Gog and Magog?

15. Read Jeremiah 49:34-39. Do you believe we are seeing these prophecies come to pass? Why or why not?

16. Read Revelation 18. Do you expect to see a literal rebuilding of the city of Babylon, as well as a flourishing of the country of Iraq? Why or why not? Are there any current signs that

Babylon will be rebuilt and Iraq will become peaceful and incredibly prosperous?

_____

_____

_____

17. Spend some time in prayer preparing your heart for Christ's return. Read Matthew 25:14-23 and ask the Lord to evaluate how you are doing with the talents He has given you.

CHAPTER THIRTY-TWO
JOIN THE REVOLUTION

"Jesus' strategy of 'love your neighbors' and 'love your enemies' is the key to winning the hearts and minds of the Muslim people, and Christians have this strategy all to themselves."
Inside the Revolution, page 494

1. How have your views or opinions about Muslims changed from what they were before you picked up this book?

   _____

   _____

   _____

2. On page 490 of *Inside the Revolution*, I ask readers to "defeat the Radicals, encourage the Reformers, and strengthen the Revivalists." What, in your view, would this involve?

   _____

   _____

   _____

   _____

3. Of the three, which seems the most urgent to you? Why?

_____

_____

_____

4. Are you serving in the military, a government security agency, or an intelligence agency? Have you ever run for public office or considered doing so? Discuss how serving in any of these capacities could help defeat the Radicals, encourage the Reformers, and strengthen the Revivalists.

_____

_____

_____

5. Brainstorm some ways you can support those who are serving in the above capacities, for example:

   - *Writing letters of encouragement to the troops*
   - *Sending care packages*
   - *Providing hospitality and practical care (babysitting, meals, etc.) to military families on the home front*
   - *Other ideas:*

_____

_____

_____

6. Do you know of any men or women fighting for reform in Muslim countries through peaceable means? If not, how might you be able to get in touch with such people?

_____

_____

_____

_____

7. Do you personally know any former Muslims who have chosen to follow Jesus Christ? Have you had the privilege of leading any Muslims to Christ yourself?

_____

_____

_____

_____

8. If there are Muslims in your community, how can you get to know them?

_____

_____

_____

_____

9. On pages 491–492, I describe my own personal journey to discover God's amazing love for the Muslim people. Where are you on such a journey?

___

___

___

___

10. Have you sensed God stirring in your heart a new or deeper sympathy and even love for your Muslim neighbors or enemies? How?

___

___

___

___

11. Take some time to read the book of Jonah in the Old Testament. It is only four chapters. Describe God's love for the people of Nineveh.

___

___

___

___

12. What are some of the reasons you think Jonah refused to obey God at first?

13. Why was Jonah mad at God in chapter 4?

14. What was God's response in Jonah 4:9-11?

15. What city in Iraq is Nineveh today? If God were to tell you to go there and preach a message of repentance at the risk of your life, would you obey? Or would you jump on a Disney cruise and head in the opposite direction? Why?

16. That said, are you ready to join the Revolution and help the Revivalists? If so, what action will you take, and what is your time frame for action?

   _____

   _____

   _____

17. What does Daniel's story on pages 508–509 tell us about Jesus' love for those willing to follow and obey Him?

   _____

   _____

   _____

18. Read Matthew 25:21. What will Jesus say to you when you stand before Him face to face?

   _____

   _____

   _____

19. What do you want Him to say to you?

   _____

   _____

   _____

20. What changes can you make—with the help of the Holy Spirit—to be sure that you will be pleasing to the Lord right up to the Day of Judgment?

21. How can you be a blessing to your family and friends so that they will live lives worthy of Jesus Christ before He comes back as well?

22. Review the Scriptures found on pages 495–498. What do these passages teach you about God's love and plan for the people of various countries in the Middle East? Going into this study, did you feel you had an in-depth understanding of God's love for Israel's neighbors? Why does the Lord love Israel's neighbors so much, and why does He want us to love them so much?

Do you sense God calling you to do something specific to love your Muslim neighbors and enemies? Would "learn, pray, give, and go" be an appropriate way for you to move forward in obedience to the Bible?

If so, review the following suggestions and make some notes about how they might apply to you and your family or friends.

LEARN
- *Study the Bible for yourself.*
- *Study the Bible with a group.*
- *Read about the people, events, and history of the Muslim world.*
- *Follow blogs and Web sites with breaking news of what's happening in the Middle East.*
- *Host a discussion group in your church or neighborhood about reaching Muslims for Christ and supporting Muslim Background Believers.*
- *Other ideas:*

_____

_____

PRAY
- *Pray about the matters listed on pages 498–499 of* Inside the Revolution.
- *Form a prayer group with other Christians concerned about Muslims.*
- *Other ideas:*

_____

_____

GIVE
- *Donate Bibles and Bible study materials, especially in epicenter languages.*
- *Donate funding for broadcast ministries operating in the Middle East.*

- *Give to humanitarian organizations and other ministries that serve in the Middle East.*
- *Support one or more full-time MBBs or NCBBs serving in a Muslim country.*
- *Support The Joshua Fund's work by going to www.joshuafund.net or sending a tax-deductible check made payable to The Joshua Fund to:*

    The Joshua Fund
    18940 Base Camp Road
    Monument, Colorado 80132-8009

- *Other ideas:*

    _____
    _____

GO

- *Share the love of Christ and hospitality with Muslim neighbors in ways suggested on pp. 503–505 of* Inside the Revolution.
- *Go on a Prayer & Vision Trip with The Joshua Fund or a similar organization.*
- *Give serious consideration to serving in a short-term ministry project in the Middle East.*
- *Research humanitarian and ministry organizations at work in the Middle East.*
- *Pray about whether God would have you serve full-time with one of these organizations.*
- *Other ideas:*

    _____
    _____

afterword

TOM DOYLE is a dear friend of mine, in part because he has a great love for all the people of the Middle East. He's traveled throughout the epicenter, sharing the gospel with Muslims and training pastors and laypeople to do the same. He also travels the United States and Canada and appears on radio and TV shows, teaching people how to love Muslims and lead them to a saving knowledge of Jesus Christ. While traveling into Afghanistan together, I asked Tom if he would write a piece for this study guide on lessons he has learned from the front lines, and he graciously agreed. May the Lord bless you as you consider his perspective and put these principles into action.

Joel C. Rosenberg

Loving Muslims to Christ
BY TOM DOYLE

TODAY, THE MUSLIM WORLD is in the midst of the most profound period of spiritual and philosophical turmoil in its fourteen-century history. *Inside the Revolution* took you behind the scenes to meet Radicals, Reformers, and Revivalists. For many of you, the question now is, how can I join the Revolution on the side of the Revivalists?

What you have to understand first and foremost is that the Revivalists are engaged in a spiritual battle of biblical proportions. The good news is that more Muslims are coming to faith in Jesus Christ than at any other time in human history. The challenge is that the Revivalists have landed squarely on the Radicals' hit list. Persecution of the Christ-followers in the Islamic world is real and it is intense. Whether they are Palestinians, Jordanians, Iraqis, or Iranians, true believers in Jesus often find themselves in a variety of frightening situations. Yet because of their faith in God, these amazing saints risk everything daily to bring the love of Jesus to their people. They have given their lives to share Christ's love within the world of Islam. It is their only hope to change anything.

International news continually highlights the latest geopolitical wars within the Muslim world, but the spiritual battle within the religion is the ultimate battle. One Arab Islamic leader thinks he has the answer to the conflict. "The leader of Libya, Muammar Qaddafi, considers himself to be a great thinker, and he announced one day that he had a solution to the problem," noted author Mark Gabriel in his book *Islam and Terrorism*. "His solution was for the Christians to convert to Islam and then they would be brothers and sisters with the Muslims and the fighting would stop. Qaddafi said: 'I hope there is a new generation of Lebanese Christians who will wake up one day and realize Arabs cannot be Christians and Christians cannot be Arabs, so then they will convert to Islam and be true Arabs.'"

Actually, many Arabs were Christians long before Islam even began, and today Arab Muslims are converting to Christianity and becoming true followers of Jesus Christ in numbers never even imagined by Church leaders over the centuries. In fact, more Muslims have come to Christ in the last ten years than in the last fourteen centuries. God has miraculously opened Muslim hearts all over the world.

You don't have to travel to the Middle East to share Jesus with a Muslim. There are several million Muslims currently living in America. There are also some 1,200 mosques in the United States. The largest mosque is the Islamic Center of America located in Dearborn, Michigan. Because of high birth rates among Muslims and a steady stream of immigration, the Islamic community is growing throughout the U.S. God has brought them to our own backyards and given us an opportunity to reach them with Jesus' love and offer of forgiveness. Muslims respect Jesus since Muhammad did, so the door is wide open to explain who Jesus is and what He taught in the Bible.

Are you willing to be used by the Lord to love Muslims to Christ? If so, here are a few principles I would highly recommend you follow:

CONFESS YOUR PREJUDICE

One problem we Westerners have with Muslims is that we often stereotype them. I know this from experience. I did it. After I had been to Israel for the first time, I was so Jewish-focused that I wouldn't give Muslims the time of day. Now as you prepare for outreach, remember most Muslims are very nice, warm people. The chances are slim that they have a bomb under their jacket. They probably don't work for Hamas. They do need Jesus, however. They will listen to you. If they are traditional and dress like seventh-century Arabs, don't let that throw you. Ask God to give you a supernatural love for Muslims. He can give you a passion to reach them. He will tenderize your heart for them. They are about 21 percent of the world's population. Your effort and participation in this world outreach program are vital.

At this point, I must confess the prejudice I had toward not only Muslims but Arabs at one time. Again, my love for Israel seemed to overshadow the needs of the Arab people. I was not drawn to them especially. I felt in some way that if I reached out to Arabs or Muslims, I was forsaking Israel. But you know what? God's love is for all people, including both Jews and Arabs. He wants Ishmael's descendants saved too. I have learned that you can love Israel—you can honor Jews and support them—and still love Arabs too. That's okay with God. Just because I believe Israel has a biblical and historical right to their land doesn't mean I can't also have a desire to reach Arabs with the gospel of Jesus.

I was in a Denver restaurant years ago, and two Arab men walked in. They both had black leather coats on and spoke with heavy Arab accents. All of this Middle East stuff was new to me, and I immediately began to judge them in my mind. *I bet they're terrorists. Maybe they've been planted in America as spies.* (Lots of other real edifying thoughts like those.) Well, wouldn't you know that the two men came and sat right next to me at another table. I began to kind of eavesdrop like Maxwell Smart or Inspector Clouseau. I felt I surely would uncover a sinister plot already under way.

I did learn a lot about them by listening to their conversation. To my shock, I soon realized that these two men were believers in Jesus! I began to hear them talk about what the Lord was doing here and what the Lord was doing there. Did I ever feel like two cents! *What a jerk you are, Tom. You judged them just because of their race.* Those thoughts ran through my mind. Then it got worse. I said hello and said, "Are you guys believers?" They said, "Yes, we're believers from Syria. Are you one too?" At that point I felt so bad that I doubted I was a believer myself. I reluctantly said, "Yes, I am." Immediately these brothers told me all about their ministry trips into Syria and how dangerous it was for them to share the gospel at home. They also worked in orphanages there. They invited me to go with them next time. Man, I was feeling worse by the minute. I had judged them. They sure didn't judge me, though. Before I knew it, one of the brothers insisted that I follow him home for coffee and to meet his wife and kids. I went and had a wonderful time. There is nothing like Arabic hospitality. These dear people were like long-lost relatives, but when I first saw them I wondered if they were safe to be around. I learned the hard way that as Americans we often carry prejudice toward Arabs and Muslims in general.

A pastor in Jerusalem asked the question one day: "What's the first thing you think of when you hear the word *Palestinian*?" The answer came quickly from our Bible tour group. "Terrorist!" He said, "Right! And if you keep that attitude, you're going to have a hard time reaching them for Jesus. Yes, there is a lot of terrorism connected with Palestinians. But we have to remember that the majority of them want nothing to do with it. And what's more, they have a soul like all other human beings. Never forget that they are also created in the image of God." Well said.

In prayer, ask God to purge you of anything that might hold you back from bringing Jesus' love to Muslims. If your heart contains anger, bitterness, and prejudice toward Muslims, you'll never reach one of them.

BEGIN A FRIENDSHIP

Muslims live in every major American city and enjoy great religious freedom here, something that is new to them if they're from the Middle East. Some Muslims, when they migrate to the West, leave some of their traditions behind. Often women and men drop the robes and burkas prevalent in Islam-controlled areas. If they do keep their traditional clothes, they probably feel somewhat isolated in the United States. It creates feelings of loneliness and they often crave friendships. After September 11, Muslims encountered much misunderstanding in our country and underwent public scrutiny. Muslims in traditional garb especially felt the stares of wondering people in public places.

I was shopping in a department store in Denver and a woman waited on me as I was shopping for my wife. She was Persian, and her accent had a familiar tone. I had to ask, "Are you from the Middle East by any chance?" She said, "Why do you ask?" I replied, "I travel there quite a bit, and I love Iranian culture. I love the people, the food, and their warmth. I was just curious." Sensing I was accepting of her, she then answered, "I'm from Iran, but I don't like to tell people that." I said, "I bet that's hard at times for you. I hope you feel welcome in America." She said, "Thank you very much." This is typical, I think.

She wasn't dressed in traditional Muslim clothes but as we visited awhile, I could tell that she was fairly open. She was approachable, also, after she realized that I appreciated her culture.

"How do I meet Muslims?" you might ask. Here are two places that you can easily meet someone of Islamic faith.

Go to a Mosque

I'm sure that I just lost some of you. *"Me, go to a mosque? Are you kidding?"* But hear me out. Most major cities in America have at least one mosque. You can go there anytime and all people are welcome. I often find a mosque and meet people there and get to know them. You can develop relationships relatively easily. I go into a mosque and pray that Jesus will open the hearts of everyone who prays there to His love and forgiveness. By the way, can you imagine what would happen if believers were doing that in all 1,200 mosques in America? I introduce myself to people and begin to find out about them. Where they are from and what they do for a living are good conversation starters. When I am asked what I am doing in a mosque as a Christian, I merely tell them that I love the people of the Middle East and I pray for them regularly. Then I follow it up by asking, "Is there anything that I can pray for you?" If you ask with a smile and a genuine heart, you won't be turned down. Who doesn't need prayer? Muslims are no different. And they won't mind that you are a Christian either.

Go Out to Eat

Since Mediterranean food and Middle Eastern food are becoming more and more popular, there are a growing number of such restaurants throughout America. These are typically family-owned eating establishments and usually run by a family from Lebanon, Jordan, or maybe even Israel. Not only is the food great but you can get to know a Muslim family in the process. Over time you can build a friendship as you support them by occasionally going to their restaurant. Get to know the family. Why not invite them over to your place for dinner and begin a friendship? They'll probably invite you to their home for the next time. You won't believe how welcoming they will be to you as their guest. Once you've been in their home and been blessed by their hospitality, you'll have friends for life.

Whether you begin a relationship in a mosque, restaurant, or wherever, pray for the Holy Spirit's leading as to when you should share your testimony about Jesus in your life.

ASK QUESTIONS

Muslims love to tell people about their religion. They hope to "set us straight" and often talk freely about their faith. Dedicated to their religion, they fail to see the huge spiritual gaps that exist within Islam. They are "good works" motivated, believing that doing good works will better their chances of going to heaven. They pray five times a day. They may even read their Qur'an, though not all do.

Yet the great spiritual chasm for Muslims is in the area of atonement. Who will pay for their sins? What sacrifice will satisfy God? What happens to their sins? Muslims have no answer to those questions. With their theology of being "justified by works," they have no certainty that they will ever make it to paradise. When it comes to terrorist acts, this is often the motivation behind the violence. The rationale for these crimes is usually to win enough points with Allah to earn salvation. In places where women have become suicide bombers, like in Israel, the motivation is usually to erase a serious offense. Women who are divorced bring disgrace to their families, and martyrdom is seen as a quick fix to restore honor.

Muslims struggle with the very same thing that all God-fearing people who don't know Christ struggle with. The question they cannot answer is whether they will have enough good works to outweigh the bad works. Will they be on the positive side of the ledger when they die? Will they build up enough equity in life to earn a place in eternity? Of course, we can show that ultimately that system breaks down, since even one sin unpaid for would exile us from heaven forever.

So after you develop a solid friendship, investigate a little. Non-threatening questions that are asked gently and not aimed at starting an argument can make them think about things. Here's one: "As Christians, we believe Jesus paid for our sins because we are incapable of doing it ourselves. What do you as a Muslim believe?"

Since Muslims believe Jesus was a prophet, ask what your friend thinks of Him. How about this question: "As a Muslim, have you ever wondered what Jesus was all about?" And later, "I would like to tell you about Him. Would you tell me all about Muhammad?"

If you ask penetrating questions in a spirit of love, the relationship will continue even if he is not ready to trust Christ as his Savior. Always remember, do not be condescending; do not argue.

PRAY MORE

If we Christians will love Muslims and build friendships with them, the doors will fling wide open for the saving power of Christ. After we have a spiritual dialogue in a calm and affirming atmosphere, the next step is most important. Get on your knees. If we pray every day for the Muslims that we know, we will see results. We will see the Holy Spirit begin to erase their misguided notions about Jesus and Christianity. We will see the Holy Spirit stirring new questions in their hearts. We will see them wanting to spend more time with us and even come to church with us. And eventually we will see Muslims pray to receive Christ with us.

But don't just pray *for* Muslims; pray *with* them, too. Muslims usually react positively when you ask them if you can pray with them right then and there. We have tried this in refugee camps in the Gaza Strip with Muslims. There are so many needs that they have. Your heart goes out to them. They often keep their eyes open when we pray because they are curious about Christians who pray with such passion. In all Middle East countries that we minister in, believers in Jesus ask Muslims how they can pray for them. Sometimes this surprises them, but since they are people who "think with their hearts," they pick up the sincerity of the believers. Usually they are more than happy to share some of the deepest struggles that they are wrestling with.

When you pray, make sure that you put your heart into it. Let the Holy Spirit fill you and the fruit of the Spirit that resonates through you will make an impact on them.

KEEP IT ON JESUS

Since Muslims believe in Jesus and have a basic respect for Him, it is not out of bounds to ask them what they think of Him. They'll probably tell you that *"Jesus is a great prophet"* or *"The Koran talks about Jesus and Muhammad praised Him."* This is all true. But now is the time to tell your Muslim friend that Jesus is the Savior of the world and that He wants to be their Savior. Don't be afraid to share this with your friend. Don't be intimidated. Paul said in the book of Romans, "I am not ashamed of the gospel, for it is the power of God for salvation to everyone who believes" (Romans 1:16). *Everyone.* This certainly applies to Muslims, right?

We have found several tools that are helpful when it comes to sharing Christ with Muslims.

Your Testimony
The personal testimony of how you came to faith in Jesus Christ and how Jesus is working in your life is powerful for Muslims. They are seeking a personal relationship with God and want one desperately. Tell your story.

The JESUS Film
The *JESUS* film on DVD has been used effectively throughout the Muslim world. It is a great visual for Muslims to get the real story about Jesus' life, death, burial, and resurrection. The *JESUS* DVD is produced by Campus Crusade, and copies are available online in many different languages and formats.

The EvangeCube
Many believers have found a great response to the EvangeCube among Muslims. This simple tool is another effective way of delivering a short visual gospel presentation. The EvangeCube is produced by e3 Partners.

Loving Muslims to Christ begins with God working in your own heart first. Then pray for Muslims, build friendships, pray with them, and finally share your faith in Jesus Christ. Don't be afraid. God *will* use you to reach them in Jesus' name. Revelation 5:9 gives us a picture of the awesome throne room of the Lamb of God. Assembled in worship are people from *every* tribe and language and people and nation who were purchased with the blood of the Lamb. Not one nation or people group will be left out. People from every religion who were set free from their sins and are now in Christ will be there too.

Many former Muslims will be there. Maybe some of them will be some of your friends—friends that you had the honor of introducing to Jesus.

Tom Doyle is a former senior pastor in Colorado Springs. He is now the Middle East director for e3 Partners. He is also the author of Two Nations under God *(B&H Publishing Group) and* Breakthrough: The Return of Hope to the Middle East *(Authentic Publishing), portions of which have been adapted for this article.*

To learn more, particularly via Joel's weblogs, please visit:

www.joelrosenberg.com
www.joshuafund.net

Please also go to www.joelrosenberg.com to sign up for "Flash Traffic" e-mails, Joel's regular geopolitical briefings and Joshua Fund project and prayer updates delivered directly to your computer or PDA.

recommended reading

ISLAM

Bernard Lewis. *What Went Wrong? The Clash Between Islam and Modernity in the Middle East*

Bernard Lewis. *The Crisis of Islam: Holy War and Unholy Terror*

John L. Esposito and Dalia Mogahed. *Who Speaks for Islam?: What a Billion Muslims Really Think*

Sayyid Qutb. *Milestones*

Vali Nasr. *The Shia Revival: How Conflicts within Islam Will Shape the Future*

V. S. Naipaul. *Among the Believers: An Islamic Journey*

Melanie Phillips. *Londonistan*

Ambassador Marwan Muasher. *The Arab Center: The Promise of Moderation*

Queen Noor of Jordan. *Leap of Faith: Memoirs of an Unexpected Life*

Benazir Bhutto. *Reconciliation: Islam, Democracy, and the West*

Ayaan Hirsi Ali. *Infidel*

Jim Murk. *Islam Rising*

Brigitte Gabriel. *Because They Hate: A Survivor of Islamic Terror Warns America*

Nonie Darwish. *Now They Call Me Infidel: Why I Renounced Jihad for America, Israel, and the War on Terror*

Karen Armstrong. *Muhammad: A Biography of the Prophet*

Robert Spencer. *The Truth About Muhammad: Founder of the World's Most Intolerant Religion*

Maulana Muhammad Ali. *Founder of the Ahmadiyya Movement*

TERRORISM AND AL QAEDA

Yaroslav Trofimov. *The Siege of Mecca: The Forgotten Uprising in Islam's Holiest Shrine and the Birth of al-Qaeda*

Lawrence Wright. *The Looming Tower: Al-Qaeda and the Road to 9/11*

Peter Bergen. *The Osama bin Laden I Know: An Oral History of al Qaeda's Leader*

Yossef Bodansky. *Bin Laden: The Man Who Declared War on America*

Randall B. Hamud. *Osama Bin Laden: America's Enemy in His Own Words*

Richard A. Clarke. *Against All Enemies: Inside America's War on Terror*

Richard Miniter. *Losing Bin Laden*

Laura Mansfield, editor. *His Own Words: A Translation of the Writings of Dr. Ayman al Zawahiri*

National Commission on Terrorist Attacks. *The 9/11 Commission Report: Final Report of the National Commission on Terrorist Attacks upon the United States*

Dore Gold. *Hatred's Kingdom: How Saudi Arabia Supports the New Global Terrorism*

Michael A. Sheehan. *Crush the Cell: How to Defeat Terrorism Without Terrorizing Ourselves*

Nicholas Noe, editor. *Voice of Hezbollah: The Statements of Sayyed Hassan Nasrallah*

Naim Qassem. *Hizbullah: The Story from Within*

UNITED STATES POLITICS

President Dwight Eisenhower. *Mandate for Change: The White House Years, 1953-1956*

President Jimmy Carter. *Keeping Faith: Memoirs of a President*

Admiral Stansfield Turner. *Burn Before Reading: Presidents, CIA Directors, and Secret Intelligence*

Zbigniew Brzezinski. *Power and Principle: Memoirs of the National Security Adviser, 1977-1981*

Henry Kissinger. *The White House Years*

Robert Gates. *From the Shadows: The Ultimate Insider's Story of Five Presidents and How They Won the Cold War*

Tim Weiner. *Legacy of Ashes: The History of the CIA*

Christopher Andrew. *For the President's Eyes Only: Secret Intelligence and the American Presidency from Washington to Bush*

George Tenet. *At the Center of the Storm: My Years at the CIA*

Bob Woodward. *State of Denial: Bush at War, Part III*

Bob Woodward. *The War Within: A Secret White House History 2006–2008*

ISLAM AND THE UNITED STATES

Mark Bowden. *Guests of the Ayatollah: The First Battle in America's War with Militant Islam*

His Majesty King Abdullah II. Address to the National Prayer Luncheon, February 2, 2006

Daniel Pipes. *Militant Islam Reaches America*

Stephen Kinzer. *All the Shah's Men: An American Coup and the Roots of Middle East Terror*

INTERNATIONAL POLITICS

Jerrold Post. *Leaders and Their Followers in a Dangerous World: The Psychology of Political Behavior*

ISRAEL

Tom Doyle. *Two Nations under God: Why You Should Care about Israel*

IRAQ

Ambassador L. Paul Bremer III. *My Year in Iraq: The Struggle to Build a Future of Hope*

James A. Baker III and Lee H. Hamilton, co-chairs. *The Iraq Study Group Report: The Way Forward—A New Approach*

CENTRAL ASIA—AFGHANISTAN AND PAKISTAN

Nick B. Mills. *Karzai: The Failing American Intervention and the Struggle for Afghanistan*

John Weaver. *Inside Afghanistan: The American Who Stayed Behind after 9/11 and His Mission of Mercy to a War-Torn People*

Pervez Musharraf. *In the Line of Fire: A Memoir*

IRAN AND THE ISLAMIC REVOLUTION

Baqer Moin. *Khomeini: Life of the Ayatollah*

Dr. Hamid Algar, translator. *Islam and Revolution 1: Writings and Declarations of Imam Khomeini (1941-1980)*

Nikki R. Keddie. *Modern Iran: Roots and Results of Revolution*

Said Amir Arjomand. *The Turban for the Crown: The Islamic Revolution in Iran*

Michael Ledeen. *The Iranian Time Bomb: The Mullah Zealots' Quest for Destruction*

William J. Daugherty. *In the Shadow of the Ayatollah: A CIA Hostage in Iran*

Ali M. Ansari. *Confronting Iran: The Failure of American Foreign Policy and the Next Great Conflict in the Middle East*

Mehdi Khalaji. *Apocalyptic Politics: On the Rationality of Iranian Policy,* Policy Focus #79, Washington Institute for Near East Policy, January 2008

Karim Sadjadpour. *Reading Khamenei: The World View of Iran's Most Powerful Leader*

Alireza Jafarzadeh. *The Iran Threat: President Ahmadinejad and the Coming Nuclear Crisis*

Yossi Melman and Meir Javedanfar. *The Nuclear Sphinx of Tehran: Mahmoud Ahmadinejad and the State of Iran*

Kasra Naji. *Ahmadinejad: The Secret History of Iran's Radical Leader*

Kenneth M. Pollack. *The Persian Puzzle: The Conflict between Iran and America*

Reza Pahlavi. *Winds of Change: The Future of Democracy in Iran*

Nasrin Alavi. *We Are Iran: The Persian Blogs*

Azar Nafisi. *Reading Lolita in Tehran*

Tom White, et al (Voice of the Martyrs). *Iran, Desperate for God: An Oppressive Islamic State Drives Its People into the Arms of Christ*

FORMER MUSLIMS AND CHRISTIAN EVANGELISM

Ibn Warraq, editor. *Leaving Islam: Apostates Speak Out*

Susan Crimp and Joel Richardson, editors. *Why We Left Islam: Former Muslims Speak Out*

Brother Andrew and Al Janssen. *Light Force: A Stirring Account of the Church Caught in the Middle East Crossfire*

Brother Andrew and Al Janssen. *Secret Believers: What Happens When Muslims Believe in Christ*

Brother Yun, Peter Xu Yongze, and Enoch Wang (with Paul Hattaway). *Back To Jerusalem: Three Chinese House Church Leaders Share Their Vision to Complete the Great Commission*

Walid Shoebat. *Why I Left Jihad: The Root of Terrorism and the Return of Radical Islam*

Tass Saada. *Once an Arafat Man: The True Story of How a PLO Sniper Found a New Life*

William McElwee Miller. *Ten Muslims Meet Christ*

Carrie McDonnall. *Facing Terror: The True Story of How an American Couple Paid the Ultimate Price for Their Love of the Muslim People*

JOEL C. ROSENBERG,
author of the *New York Times* best seller *Epicenter*, brings readers inside the Revolution.

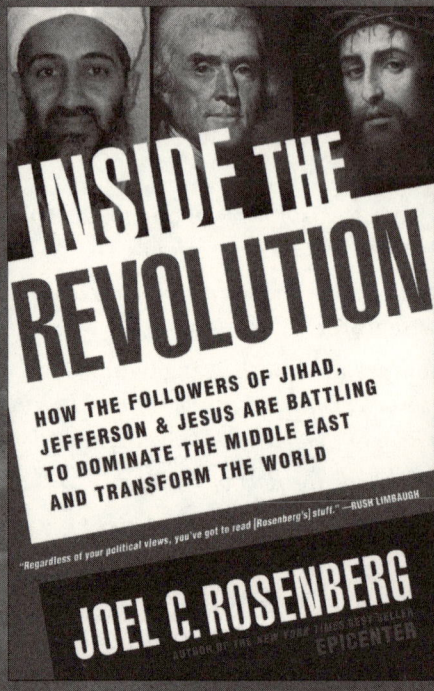

Rosenberg argues there are now three movements poised to change the world forever, for good or for ill.

Joel C. Rosenberg takes you inside the Revolution in this compelling documentary based on the *New York Times* best-selling book.

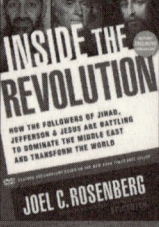

Now available in stores and online.

"Rosenberg has become one of the most **entertaining** and **thought-provoking** novelists of our day. Regardless of your political views, you've got to read his stuff."
>> RUSH LIMBAUGH

★ ★ ★

★ ★ ★

WWW.JOELROSENBERG.COM